Stoic Living for the Modern Soul

DMITRI MANDALIEV

ISBN: 1496191242
ISBN-13: 978-1496191243

INSPIRATION

"...*to have contemplated human life for forty years is the same as to have contemplated it for ten thousand years. For what more wilt thou see?*" -Marcus Aurelius

"*And what is it which this reason demands of him? The easiest thing in the world, - to live in accordance with his own nature. But this is turned into a hard task by the general madness of mankind; we push one another into vice. And how can a man be recalled to salvation, when he has none to restrain him, and all mankind to urge him on?*" -Seneca

CONTENTS

1   Book One: Introduction   1

2   Book Two: Regarding the body   11

3   Book Three: Regarding the mind   19

4   Book Four: Regarding the spirit   29

5   Book Five: Regarding the living of life   31

BOOK ONE: INTRODUCTION

1. Life is habits. The quality of life one has corresponds directly to the habits one keeps. Some live a life devoid of any distinguishable habits and are ruled by chaos. Others live a life of destructive habits which over time chip away at the mind, the spirit, and the body. If you fall prey to desire, casting aside reason and virtue, you will erode the most important gift that you're given at birth. By turning your back on this gift you harm yourself and those around you. Reason is the guiding star you must train your sights on lest you lose your way. Virtue is the rope you must cling to lest you fall into the abyss. Stoicism shows us such a star and offers us such a rope.

While this book centers around stoicism I must make clear that my view of stoicism and the image of it that I present in this book is not dogmatic. I will not discuss logic and physics. The ethics of stoicism and the influence it has had on my life are the central features which are most important to me.

I consider stoicism as a philosophy to be flexible, malleable, and able to be absorbed and molded to one's life. In this way I am an eclectic stoic rather than a pure stoic. I would argue that ideals and ethics are living and breathing things which move with us through the ages—that they are hardly static and immovable things. It is from this perspective that I call this book Stoic Living for the Modern Soul. It is my belief that people of our age may live better, without trying to exist in some unbending and dogmatic, stoic way. For example, some may take stoic teachings so literally as to try and avoid their emotions. I feel that to try and adhere to a lack of emotion is actually harmful and unrealistic for a human being. I should point out that I am scarcely new in being skeptical of certain features of dogmatic stoicism. In this way I follow in the footsteps of men such as Herodes Atticus. It might be said that I follow in the footsteps of

Seneca himself, or Marcus Aurelius, as neither could scarcely be called dogmatic in their stoicism. I would be content to keep such company.

So, from this perspective I must continue with a question:

What is stoicism?

This book will not be a history of the philosophy or a going over of technical terms. I will not make this an academic exercise of discussing Greek words like *apatheia*. I have no desire for you to read this book and have merely an intellectual grasp over history and terminology. I assume that you are reading this book because you have some understanding of what stoicism is. Additionally, this book will not simply parrot ancient philosophy, though I naturally concur with much of what it says. This work is primarily drawn from my understanding of what stoicism is and how it has been a positive influence on my life. It will present a picture of stoicism as I live it, with instruction on stoicism as a way to live. I instruct myself in this way of life and share it with you as a fellow traveler.

This work aims to show you what/when/how stoic approaches to life may be useful. I will endeavor to correct what I think are some misunderstandings and caricatures of stoicism which one often encounters. In brief, I write this work as a modern stoic, who lives and breathes. In order to answer the question "What is stoicism?" I can only report from what my eyes, spirit, and experience have told me.

Stoicism can be a mental exercise or it can be a way of life to be embraced. Those who choose to embrace it live close to their virtue and reason. As Seneca has put it, virtue itself is right reason. A stoic life may offer a beacon of hope in a dark world largely ruled by fears and desires. Yet stoicism is misunderstood and might be any number of other things. So what is stoicism, exactly? Stoic philosophy can be used like a map or the guidance of stars. It reminds us of the path— it's not the path itself. Only by looking within may we find our path. Ultimately I arrive at the following definition:

Stoicism is a psychological state of mind which embraces the attributes of inner harmony and accord over inner dissonance and struggle.

It is the state of mind of one who is tranquil and yet ready to respond to crises and difficulties. It is the perspective of one who understands the troubles of life and deals with them as best possible. This is achieved through self-knowledge and acceptance. At any point in life one may turn to one path (response) or the other. Through practice, experience, and especially failure, we may develop habits which will keep us on the right course. When we embrace these new habits we take on new characteristics.

What are some characteristics of a stoic?

2. Does a stoic have feelings? Is a stoic never moved by what happens to them or those they care for? One often reads that stoics are cold and lack feeling. To believe that stoics are robotic and unfeeling is a grave misunderstanding. A stoic may have the goal of not being tossed about on the sea of his emotions, to be in control of his state, and to rule over himself. Yet, in order to achieve this the stoic doesn't suppress feelings. This is where many go wrong in trying to understand stoicism and why they give up on the philosophy after a trial period. The truth is that a stoic's perspective and emotional state is born out of acceptance for reality, however harsh that reality may be. Does your child or spouse die? Do you really believe you could have no feelings of pain or remorse for such a thing? If you fight your feelings and suppress them they will rule over you. Emotions will have their day, it is just a matter of time. However, they do not need overrun you. A stoic will sit with these feelings, allow them to sink in and not struggle with them. This is a painful experience. Yet from this pain comes strength, resilience, and ultimately self-control.

This may seem like a paradox or contradiction, yet this is how the human animal operates. Modern psychological therapies like CBT (Cognitive Behavioral Therapy) and ACT (Acceptance and Commitment Therapy) have their roots in stoic philosophy and have done a great deal to document the ways in which confronting, feeling, and accepting one's anxieties, hurts and fears can actually lead to greater health and stability. Rather than running away from anxieties and grief, a stoic embraces them with what is sometimes called 'stoic calm'. That is to say, unflinchingly, and without histrionics. It's no accident that modern psychological advice so often echoes the great stoic works of writers like Seneca, Epictetus, and Marcus Aurelius. Unfortunately, for many the words of these authors are taken too literally and the message is lost, disfigured, or diluted.

I put it to you that a stoic has feelings and is in touch with them perhaps more than most people. This is so because the stoic confronts and accepts their reality in as fearless a way as is possible. And when the stoic fails, they do not wail and bemoan their error. The stoic picks himself up off the ground and marches forward, acknowledging the error as well as the fact that he is human.

3. Are stoics pessimists, fatalists, or pessimistic fatalists? There is a temptation to take the stoic viewpoint as being pessimistic. To a certain degree stoics are fatalists but not to the degree that some might suggest. On the face of things, stoic philosophy teaches acceptance of many things, including troubles and inequities. A cornerstone of stoic philosophy is that the primary thing one can control in life is one's perspective. In fact, stoic writers often talk about not avoiding any thing because there is no reason to. To a stoic there is literally, "nothing either good or bad, but thinking makes it so." (That Hamlet is littered with stoic philosophy is one of the reasons it is such a great work.) Yet, at the same time Marcus Aurelius urges us to avoid false friends. How can this contradiction be? If we are to accept everything then perhaps we are fatalists. Yet, if we are to take some action in our life, to steer ourselves by following our true nature and guiding principle, then we cannot be complete fatalists. If we avoid false friends or other situations that would harm us then we cannot ascribe to being totally fatalistic.

Neither can we be pessimists if we do our utmost to adhere to virtue in the face of our adversities. If we believe that things will always turn out for the worse, what reason do we have to aim for a better course of action? How easy it is to turn your back on virtue when you see an opportunity to better your situation. How easy it is to turn your back on virtue when your desires call you. If we are pessimists and fatalists, what reason would we have to strive to live by reason and virtue? I submit that a stoic cannot be a pessimist. If a stoic is a fatalist, it is only insofar as he believes that all things occur for some reason—meaning that the guiding principle of nature moves throughout all things and all actions. Yet, a stoic doesn't see that as an excuse to behave recklessly, giving into desires and fears. Neither does the stoic see it as an excuse to withdraw and fail to take action when necessary. One cannot simultaneously abdicate and also hold oneself accountable for the impact one has on the world. A stoic understands his responsibilities and does not shirk them.

Do stoics avoid all comfort?

4. It could be fairly said that a man who has embraced a stoic way of life has learned that he is capable of enduring much hardship—that he can do without many things of which he once felt certain were necessities. If you have a comfortable bed, yet wish to lay on the floor from time to time, do so, but do not destroy the bed—there is no reason in that. As Epictetus talks of accepting what comes to you in life as at a banquet, there is nothing stoic about purposefully creating an intolerable environment for oneself where none exists. Pushing away something that is offered to you is no more stoic than taking something from someone else that you wish to have. Regarding comforts, the issue in most cases is moderation: a stoic understands the middle path. Take your part of what is offered, even if it be a comfort that is offered, but do not demand more. To strive to better oneself is admirable. To strive to do better at one's work is admirable. To strive to be more virtuous and to adhere more to one's reason are both admirable. To humbly accept what is given to you and to show your appreciation are admirable. Taking food from another's plate is not.

What about passion? Does a stoic feel any passion for life?

5. Many will turn away from stoicism because they are bound up in the pleasures of life and view stoicism as rejecting life's pleasures. Yet is this so? Certainly, a stoic aim is not to allow desires or fears to control you. This means controlling the appetite for sex as much as

for food and drink. It means ceasing to compare one's wealth to others'. It means no more striving to catch up with them. It also means checking one's appetites when they threaten to lead you into the abyss.

However, there is much in life to feel passion and joy for. Passion for one's family, one's work, one's community, for knowledge, self-improvement, and for virtue and reason themselves. The difference is whether or not one's ego is the driving force behind the passion. Do you crave more sex because it will make you feel more whole? Do you eat, not because you are hungry, but because you have a void to fill? Is your aim in your work to achieve praise from others, and fame? A man who embraces stoicism may enjoy his meals, but for different reasons than he had before. Perhaps his joy is in sharing his meal with others, or in the act of appreciating satiating of true hunger over psychological hunger. Sex is no longer something that he needs in order to feel whole. It becomes something that is a joy to share with another, or perhaps just a physical release such as are commonplace to the human animal. In either case the stoic lives— but lives differently—with different meaning ascribed to the activities.

The ego is gradually dismantled by a stoic life. It is still present, but rather than being the driver it is in the back seat, or the trunk, or left at home. True enjoyment of the passions of life is incompatible with ego gratification. The ego is never satisfied and will lead to self-destruction. Only by taming it are we free to truly enjoy life. One way to do so is through stoic living and so it offers a path to more engaged living.

6. There are many attributes of a stoic that could be discussed, but the primary point is that stoicism may not be what we may have supposed. It is not an ivory tower into which one disappears to turn away from life. On the contrary, it is embracing life in a manner more fully than one had before. To face the anxieties, pain, and suffering in such a way as to no longer be controlled by them is truly liberating. To engage in eating, sex, exercise, and work in more meaningful and straightforward ways is empowering and removes extraneous psychological clutter from one's existence. I put it to you that to live

a stoic life is to embrace a clear ray of sunshine in what was once a dark pit. This pit was one we created ourselves, fueled by our endless yearnings to appease a fragile ego. Modern life has become centered on feeding one's ego. In our modern age we enjoy creature comforts the likes of which most who have lived before us never knew. Yet we are dissatisfied on the whole with life. It is due to our lack of understanding and feeding of our ego that we have become so lost. Stoic living pats that ego on the head and puts it to bed. When the ego appears again, we treat it fairly, but we always put it back to bed.

Is stoicism rigid?

7. Stoicism is more flexible and dynamic than we might suppose. Each human being has his own nature to follow. We are all connected to what Marcus Aurelius called, 'The Universal', and achieving our full potential takes us on a very different path than we'd been on before. Incidentally, I should point out that discussions of God, The Universal, and so forth, in reference to stoicism should be taken with a grain of salt. To meander into a debate about belief versus non-belief would derail one from one's course, as would discussion of political correctness. Ultimately, whether or not we disintegrate, are extinguished, or are re-formed into something else is not the central issue of human life. After all, that is a question about something which has yet to happen to you: Death. Death will come, but it is not yet at hand. To illustrate, I will paraphrase Marcus Aurelius, Epictetus, and Seneca:

On either side of us is an ocean of time. On one side is the past, which is lost to us; on the other is the future, which is uncertain. The only certain thing is the present moment.

How we live in this present moment is up to us, and stoicism does not posit that there is one particular way to do so 'correctly'. There are no vows of celibacy. One need not give up all of one's possessions and live in a monastery. One need not pray daily to a deity. Marcus Aurelius has the following to say, which is as good, rough and concise of a guides as you may find:

The perfection of moral character consists in this, in passing every day as the last, and in being neither violently excited nor torpid nor playing the hypocrite. And:

Do not act as thou wert going to live ten thousand years. Death hangs over thee. While thou livest, while it is in thy power, be good.

There is no one correct way to follow such advice, just as there is no one correct way to live a stoic life. The philosophy is flexible and adaptable to any situation because it is not concerned with specifics. In every situation we have the opportunity to, 'be good', as Marcus Aurelius suggest. What this means from day to day, from hour to hour, is not measured by one set of rules. There are no commandments to adhere to. What one must learn to adhere to is one's inner nature, the voice that we are imbued with if we will listen to it. An equally important and powerful part of what he says is that we not play the hypocrite. In this way, Marcus Aurelius reminds us that, while we are to listen to our inner voice, we must not take advantage of it so that we may do ill, claiming all the while that we are following our inner nature. For while we may commit an ill blindly and out of ignorance, to do so willingly and with knowledge would make us hypocrites.

8. As a young man I drifted into a life of chaos, pain, and disillusionment. In my thirties I began a quest to rise up out of my confusion and error. Stoicism has been a key part of my transformation: from a lost and broken man to one who has made a kind of peace in his life. I endeavor to share with you what I have learned in these last forty years. This is my account, my understanding, my way. It is imbued with lessons of the past, yet it is my own. There is no single correct way. It is important that you understand and accept this. You and I are different, as much as we are the same.

I have found the stoic way of life to be an exceptionally satisfying one. Perhaps more importantly: it's a way of life which leads us to fulfill our ultimate potential. Our potential is to be human, in every sense of the word. A chief aim of stoicism is to be more man than beast—sticking to reason and virtue is the way. We fall and fail, yet we must get back up and soldier on. And what is the goal of this endeavor, if not to live better?

What is living better?

9. To live better is to live more fully, to remove impediments from our way. It is a life of right reason and virtue. To cast aside our preference for comforts and consumption, to take what looks like a difficult path when we know it to be the right one. To be right is to stand upright. How can your shoulders hunch under a burden of guilt or shame if you stand erect in confidence of your behavior? Mankind so often huddles in the dark, scheming revenge for slights real and imagined. How often have you found yourself cursing others, or yourself, for your lot? How often have you had impulse to raise your hand to your boss, your spouse, or your children? When these passions stir you, you must work to correct and rule yourself. It is not enough to merely control yourself while a tide of trouble builds behind your defenses. You must wade out, far away from your murky shore and work. These urges to harm others erode your being, therefore, you must get to their roots and pull them out.

This is not to say that there is a life possible without troubles. Quite the contrary, the good life may be filled with more troubles than a life which is filled with evils. That life has troubles is a given. How much evil is done in seeking to end all troubles and lash oneself permanently to a bed of pleasure? The world is filled with such wrongdoing. Whether intentions be good or not is unimportant. If we mean well and cause a harm, the harm stands. Is it the right way to try and squirm out of our responsibility by saying, "Yes, but I meant well"? To live a good life means being honest with ourselves, first and foremost. No more childish games and rationalizations. No more squeamishness for doing what we must do. When we determine the right path we march forward without complaint.

10. Determining what actions to take in life can be difficult. A stoic aim is to live according to your true nature, according to your human reason, and according to virtue. To do so requires effort, trial, and error. Each man knows internally when he's done wrong, though some have built up such defenses to these signals that they never see them. Some misread these signals as signs that they are on the right

path. Some see virtue and reason as weaknesses. As a stoic you must leave behind prior judgments and dependence on the opinion of others. This is often incompatible with how many live their lives. Constantly seeking validation, acceptance, and approval is commonplace and yet, a roadblock to one's development. In each situation you encounter in your life you will have options. Of these options one will be calling out to you more than the others. Yet is this always the correct path? What if the voice is driven by fear? By a desire for approval, pleasure, or power over others? How well do you know yourself to distinguish between these?

Learning the difference between your inner voice of reason and that of the demons that chase you (or which you chase) is part of the process of living a stoic life. There is no end point at which you have arrived, and after which, there is no more work or growth to be done. It is more of a stance, or a style of walking than a destination at which you stop moving. Time marches forward, and you with it. You succeed, fail, learn, and grow. I will impart some of what I can to help. And of course if I have anything worthy at all to say it is because I have steeped myself for many hours in the works of great men who have long before me put down their wisdom for us all.

What will you get out of reading this book?

A year into writing this book I found myself at an impasse. I was depressed and felt I had somehow lost my way. The details aren't important, suffice it to say I was feeling low. I hadn't looked at this piece for a while and decided I could at least make use of some down time by editing it. While I read, removing extraneous bits and hopefully correcting egregious errors, something unexpected happened: I felt inspired. While a great deal of this work was written to myself as reminders of things I've learned, I hadn't actually picked it up to read it. In doing so, I was reminded of a great many positives and it helped turn my frame of mind around. It is my hope that in reading this book you may find some inner strength to meet challenges which you perhaps may have forgotten about. Further, I hope that you may develop stoic practices which aid you in living a productive, and useful, modern life.

BOOK TWO: REGARDING THE BODY

1. Your body is the temple you live in, the vehicle you travel in, and the tool you act with in this world. Ultimately it is what connects you to all other things. When you breathe, you mingle that which is yours with that which is outside of you. In those moments when you take in air, the air becomes you as you become the air. When kissing another your moisture mingles with theirs, your cells mingle with theirs—in that moment you are joined. When you hear the words spoken by another the sound carries across the air and moves your eardrum. In that moment you perceive the content and message, the intention and insight of this other, and you mix with them. Your brain responds, making meaning of the sounds which are spoken, assuming you have learned their language. When you see someone walking, talking, or gesturing with their body, you learn from this motion what it is that they mean to communicate. In this way your eyes perceive the light which reflects off of their body. Your brain responds and creates the pictures and meanings, often filling in blanks or adding its own flourishes to their act. In this way you mingle with their action and by interpreting it you become part of it, if only for a moment.

All beings are connected in this way, through the mechanisms which nature has deemed appropriate to construct. We are connected to animals, to plants, to all things. How often we feel separated and isolated from our fellow beings? What pains are taken to numb all of the senses which would connect us to the outside world? Consider the damage done to ourselves and to our world when we violently cut ourselves off with drink, food, drugs, and by other means we might call 'intellectual'.

It's understandable that humans would recoil from nature, especially from other men. The horrors that mankind has unleashed on itself and on nature are astounding. Yet our capacity for connection remains even in the face of unspeakable horrors. Is there not something curious about the human animal that we retain our ability for intimacy with others even when we might otherwise shut down and withdraw completely? Does it not speak to an inherent strength of spirit and resilience? Yet, we also have the capacity to engage in the most anti-social and depraved of behaviors.

With this in mind we might ask ourselves, what is the ruling principle which guides us along the way? Are we to allow our bodies to be the ultimate arbiter of our actions? Should our direction from waking to sleep be taken from the body alone?

2. Your body is a vessel, yet your intellect and reason must be the guide. To let one's body rule and guide itself without oversight can lead to its destruction. The body is as a child that needs its parents to establish its habits, rules, and goals before it is able to do so itself. Look around you and it will be easy to see those whose bodies run amok, unguided by reason and sound judgment. You may even see this in yourself if you look closely and without bias.

So, how might one establish habits and rules for the body—and what should those rules be? Sloth and gluttony are habits which cause the body to soften and ripe. Therefore, these are two enemies which you must assess and meet head on if you are to establish rule over your body. Allow either to get a foothold and your task to remove them will be tenfold more difficult. We must also avoid habitual use of drink and other drugs. If you have any issues with drugs, including habitual use of tobacco, that must be addressed firstly. You cannot create any lasting control over your body while you continually submit your mind to its cravings. You will ever be its slave. Lastly, rest is of paramount importance. The man who overlooks his need for rest does so at his own peril.

Each body has its own needs and wants for food and drink. We've been told a lie that all bodies require the same types of nutrients and in the same amounts. Yet we know that each body may tolerate nutrients differently than others. Therefore your first task is to understand what it is that your body tolerates and works with well.

This may take time and effort, but it is better to expend the energy to learn what your body requires than to follow rote laws blindly and cause your body harm. Some people will not tolerate carbohydrates as well as others—they will need to limit the amount of carbohydrates that they take each day. (And so on. There is no point to list all nutrients, the idea extrapolates to all.)

So, having established what your body tolerates, and what it doesn't, you need to take aim at your relationship with food. Gluttony is a powerful enemy and requires vigilance and a firm hand. For many, the problems of the body stem from an unhealthy relationship with food. They find themselves eating when they feel bored, or when they feel they should eat, rather than eating when they are truly hungry and in need of nourishment. Some reward themselves with food when they feel they have earned the right to be gluttonous. In fact, it seems built into our culture: when we reach another year in age we're expected to gorge on cake, ice cream, and other treats, while our friends and family join in. The list of occasions in which we reward ourselves with copious amounts of food is extensive. Those who resist these rituals are often maligned as being anti-social. Yet, you must be vigilant against this pressure and adhere to your reason. And if you succumb, do not beat yourself up over the transgression—simply move forward and do your best at the next opportunity.

Yet we must begin by treating every day as our opportunity to take in what food we need rather than eating out of anxiety, celebration, or the feeling that it's time to eat. A good starting point is fasting. A period spent with water only will teach your body what true hunger is, if you've forgotten. There is no correct period to fast for. To begin with, try skipping a meal. The point is not to reach some benchmark of time, but to relearn what you have forgotten.

Time is a factor: we should keep watch over how often we are eating. It is of paramount importance that you not eat too frequently, just as it is important that you not eat too much at each meal. Your body needs time to burn through the fuel which you give it. In this way your body is like a stove. Do you put more wood in than the stove can hold and burn at one time? Do you shove wood into the stove so often that you extinguish the fire that burns there? There is a fire in your belly, a fire which burns and needs time to get through what you've given it. Remember that you cause your body harm when you eat before it is ready. There is no set time to wait, as it depends on your body and the amount of food you've eaten, and its composition. Yet give yourself about five hours at least unless you have eaten some tiny amount. Learn to feel real hunger, as you may have forgotten. Also, remember to chew your food thoroughly.

Do not eat soon before bed. Allow at least three hours before you sleep at night so that your body may digest what you have given it. Aim to have twelve hours (at least) between your last meal of the day and your first the next day. This is a rough guide of course, but in doing so you will ensure that your body can use the fuel you have given it. You will also give the body ample opportunity to burn excess fat which you may have stored.

Remember to drink plenty of water each day. Warm or hot water is best though at times cooler water is okay. Staying hydrated is good for health and consuming water will keep your appetite in check. Eight cups or so of water per day is a good target. Do not drink too late into evening as it may cause you to have to wake many times in the night to urinate.

3. In doing these things your body will go through changes. And in this course of events your mind will also change. When confronted with hunger your body will reach out to your mind for lenience and try to convince you to give into your old habits. You must hold fast. Take joy and comfort in the newfound mastery of your body. Reward your mind by focusing on the fact that you are now in control. More importantly, remind yourself that what you are doing is ultimately for your own benefit. Especially if you are trying to shed stubborn fat, remember that your body must adjust to burn this fat. When the pain of hunger reaches you, think to yourself,

This hunger is proof of my mastery over my body. The discomfort I feel now is the consequence of my improved health and should be welcomed.

The transformation is its own reward. As you grow leaner and in more command of your habits and impulses your confidence in yourself and your decision making will grow as well. This is not to be underestimated, nor undervalued. Over time you will see tangible changes in how you operate day to day and how you live. This is an important step. From taking hold of your eating habits and appetite for food you establish a foothold: you are in command of your actions; you decide what you will do and not do. There are numerous software applications which may help you track your nutrient and caloric intake. Use these until such time as you have established new habits.

Each morning you may devise an eating plan for the day if you wish. In the beginning this is better than leaving things up to chance. Later it may be okay to simply listen to your body, but you must learn to distinguish true signals of hunger from psychological hunger if you have confused the two.

If you are hungry in the morning when you wake, eat. Eat until you are full and then stop eating. Use your judgment. Determine if it is better to eat a late lunch or go the whole day until it is time for dinner. Two meals per day is often enough. If you become comfortable with this way of living you will know a feeling a freedom from appetite that is rare and rewarding.

Make your decision about when to eat and hold to it unless absolutely necessary to do otherwise. At the end of the fasting period you will have pushed your boundaries and held firm to a goal. This is an important thing which you can do daily. Food is just one aspect of your life which you can apply this to. The movement of your body is another.

4. Sloth dulls your body and mind. Do you find yourself sedentary too often? Do you sit at every opportunity? Do you never walk or take the stairs? Notice how your body feels when you are too often immobile. Notice the effect it has on your mind. Exercise is important for the body as well as the mind. They work in tandem. As you increase your body's resilience and stamina, so the effect is carried forward to your mind.

Your body was made to move about the world and to work. To stay passive too often makes one more cow than human being. Embrace your body and begin to be more active. To begin with, find ways to move more. If you must sit all day at your work, and are unable to arrange a standing workstation, make a point to stand as often as is possible.

Do not engage in mindless activity. Be active to a purpose. If you run, do not run daily and constantly as it will wear your joints down until they are brittle. Instead, sprint once a week or so. Obviously, the younger you are the more you will bristle at such advice. Yet, from the hindsight of my forty years I tell you that running so often serves little purpose but to give you an endorphin rush and to weaken your body. Rather than running every day, walk daily in a brisk manner. If you are able to walk to work, do so, and take stairs whenever possible. The chief thing is to move rather than stay still for long periods. If you must stay still for long periods, endeavor to stand or squat rather than sit.

Engage in resistance training a few times a week. Do not mindlessly lift weights every day with no progress. Push yourself and you will reap rewards. For men in particular, resistance training is key as we get older, but it is worthwhile to begin such habits when we are younger. Aside from added strength and confidence, there are hormonal boosts that are good for you, including testosterone. Do not work just one part of your body to exclusion. Begin by lifting your own weight, whether it be using a pull up bar or pushups. Do not neglect your core and do planks or leg lifts. Your core is what holds you erect and it is important to keep your core engaged throughout the day, particularly when standing. This will help keep your back healthy.

The important thing is to develop a fitness program and stick to it. There are many who are more qualified than I to help you develop a sane and workable plan. Remember that life is habits. If you develop good habits for fitness you will carry forward with your program when you are tempted into sloth. In this way your mind takes over the stewardship of the body when it tempts otherwise. And sometimes the body is so driven by its habit for activity that it can guide a mind that may be distracted. Do not overdo things. It is important that if you are exhausted you should rest rather than over exerting and injuring yourself.

If you are trying to lose body fat: in measuring your progress do not rely on weight scales as they are unpredictable and often inaccurate. Are you measuring body fat, water, or muscle? Instead, use a measuring tape around your belly. Measure the same place multiple times to ensure you get an accurate measurement.

5. Sleep. How much sleep do you get typically? I wager that in our modern age most do not get the sleep that their bodies require. There is no magic number of hours of sleep one needs, but if you are tired throughout the day and are increasingly so throughout your week, you need more rest. Some important facts to remember. You cannot build muscle unless you are getting adequate rest. Or to put it more accurately, you won't build as much muscle if you aren't resting properly. Your muscles build when they recover from the stress you put on them, not while you are stressing them. Another fact is that your brain requires sleep. Your hormones and every other part of your human animal are thrown off when you do not get proper rest. Further, it's harder to lose fat if you don't get proper rest because of hormone problems.

If you are under slept, endeavor to sleep earlier. If you are a light sleeper it may be necessary to use earplugs or a cover for your eyes. As far as is possible, do not wake with an alarm but allow your body to wake naturally. This may be a struggle, yet, your body can adjust to waking at the same time each day. Sunlight will help you to wake, as will a false sunrise lamp. In winter these can be quite useful as we find ourselves needing to wake before dawn to get to work.

One problem that many have is in falling asleep. I myself have long struggled with this problem. Use of caffeine or other stimulants during the day may cause you to have trouble sleeping. I recommend no more than one cup of coffee and/or tea in the morning. Afternoon caffeine can play havoc with your sleep. To assist with sleeping I've used various supplements at times, like melatonin, which works well. However, I do not recommend that you use it constantly. Often, I have stayed awake past the point when my body was ready to sleep (yawning and about to pass out) and then later when I've tried to sleep my body has resisted. It's taken me a long time to learn: when your body tells you it is ready to sleep it is then time to sleep. If at all possible to adhere to your body's signals, do so. A good idea to focus on while you are ready to sleep is,

I have done enough for today and have done my best. It is now time to take my rest.

If you find yourself less than functional during the day, endeavor to rest. If this is not possible make a plan to get to sleep earlier that night. Leave nothing to chance and set a bedtime. Wind yourself down an hour or so before the time to sleep. Turn off all electronic devices. Stretch or do some breathing exercises. Read a book. Meditate. This is an excellent time to take an inventory of your day, so long as you not obsess over some detail to the point of remaining awake. It may be an even better use of your time to empty your mind and visualize yourself getting good rest. Or, imagine yourself going down a winding staircase which disappears into darkness. As you reach each step, count. One, two, three, and so on. Another thing to try is to imagine someone sleeping next to you (if there is not already) and that may help you to fall asleep.

6. Your body has a way of keeping accord with its habits, whether they be good or bad. This is why you must make your body subservient to your mind and establish healthy habits. If the body mutinies it is essential that you gain control. I put it to you that this is the most important thing as you begin to better your relationship with your body, for how can you make progress if your mind and body are at war with one another?

BOOK THREE: REGARDING THE MIND

1. What is a man without his mind? What dreams may he have, what actions may he take, and what life might he live without a mind? Your mind is everything. It is the window through which you see the world. Yet, it is much more than a passive window, as we shape all that we see and imbue it with our own character and prejudice. Keeping a healthy and agile mind cannot be stressed enough. Neither can it be overemphasized that one must develop one's reasoning faculty. It is through this faculty that we find virtue and the means to live the good life.

To know oneself is a primary goal of a stoic. To shine a light on one's thoughts and actions in order that you may see yourself clearly. To achieve such a perspective is worth more than any fortune. Yet, over time we change. We can look back over our past and see how we once deluded ourselves. We must then ask ourselves if we are seeing truly and clearly now. We must be vigilant as we are ever able to deceive ourselves, even more so than we can deceive others. It is our mind which allows both of these, so we must take special care with regard to its use. Whether we fashion it for truth or delusion is our choice.

Like the body, the mind must be exercised and kept fit. You must look at yourself each day and hold yourself to a high standard. As you develop habits in this you will be better able to stay true and keep yourself honest. And yet, again, we all change throughout time. We may not know today what tools we will need tomorrow in order to keep ourselves humble and true. This is why we embrace principles. To develop particular routines only would be a failure. Our principles adapt and can be extrapolated to our changing life circumstances. Through our principles we are able to remain true to ourselves and thus true to the universal in us as well as our fellow man.

Part of remaining true is in embracing a stoic philosophy and lifestyle on a deeper level than the surface. To embrace it on a surface level only, for the purpose of vain discussions with others, is an aberration and serves the ego's need for gratification. One might think, "Oh, look how stoic I've become", yet fail one's self and one's fellow men at every turn. Further, you will find that to embrace the stoic ideals with your mind in a superficial way will fail you. Doing so will not yield the result you were seeking. In fact it may harm you. As the saying goes, use a blade with two edges with great care.

2. How then to cultivate one's mind? Let your starting point be humility. If you are successful, by our measurements of success, recognize how easily it might have been otherwise. Look to the events of your life and see how Fortune has favored you. Then recognize that your success may have been your undoing. What is it that you seek? Is it praise and riches? If you already have these, and are not fulfilled, then you know the hollowness of that kind of triumph. You also know how easily all of those things might be taken from you. The adoration of crowds evaporates as quickly as it appears. Does your wealth represent the best of what you are? Can anyone say, "Look at him, he has so much, he must be a great man!"? And yet, people do say such things out of foolishness. Enlighten your mind to the realization that the shroud you cover yourself with is worthless. Whether you have the finest clothes, the finest of cars, the finest of everything, these things mean nothing. Can you accept this and be humble? Until you are ready to accept this you will circle the drain of your own delusion and misery—and no man may help you.

This is not to say that you should dump all of your clothes, riches, and car into the river. That would be equally foolish and without reason. The issue is how your mind confronts and assesses the value of the objects in your possession, for they are just objects. Men are not objects, yet often treat each other as such. Do you do so? It would scarcely be honest to answer that you do not. For we all do at one time or another. Yet we must catch ourselves each time we have this impulse and recognize that the person we see as an object is in fact a human being. The man in the street who approaches us for money. The tyrant who rules over us at the office. These are people, though we would have them abused in one form or another. And if you are the tyrant at the office, those who you treat as your playthings, they are human beings. You are less than they when you shuffle them about as pieces on a board. Whether you are tyrant or slave, think on the other. Imagine that they go home to families, that they have dreams, ambitions, and hopes as do you. This is a first step: to put yourself in another's place.

Humility is born when we recognize our faults and weaknesses. When we see how alike we are to our fellow man, though we may have dreamed otherwise, we return to a source of our understanding. Most of us are slaves of one sort or another, though we do not recognize this fact. Our masters rule over us, though we may have no physical chains. We are ruled nonetheless. How eager are we to put others into chains as well? How eager are we to judge others? As we go through life the opportunities to judge and enslave others present themselves with regularity. The great man will check his own desires for power over others and focus instead on gaining power over himself.

3. Freedom is available to you at any moment. Your mind is capable of providing a release from what torments you. But be careful that you not use your mind to escape, for there is no freedom in that. Only when we confront our torments and embrace them may we be free of them. It is in the running and avoidance of those things that they catch us and hold us fast. However we squirm, we are caught and going nowhere.

Begin by understanding what it is that you fear, what it is that you are angry with, and what it is that you desire to the point of pain. Have you lost something? Is there something you wish to gain? Perhaps your childhood was filled with terrors. Perhaps you have spent most of your life, including your adult life, running from the painful memories of your childhood. You've engaged in drugs, sex, relationships, travel, and perhaps even artistic endeavors, all to escape the history and painful truths. To be sure, you must have mercy on yourself. There is no sense in blaming yourself for your escapism. There is no wisdom in judging yourself for coping with your pain in the best way you have known. Yet, it also makes no sense to continue to engage in such methods when they do not work. It is foolish to continue when these means only serve to harm you further and to further alienate you from your fellow men.

4. Begin by imagining what it is that troubles you. Embrace the pain of the memories. This may take much time and cause grief. You may think of it as opening wounds. If it helps to heal you, so be it. A therapist may help you get through this process and there is no shame in seeking one out. But take care—if anyone seeks to help you escape your pain by some cognitive means, it is still escapism. What you need is an acceptance of what has happened to you so that you may move forward and stop living under its shadow.

As you imagine what is troubling you, you must also feel the feelings that come. This is the painful part. Perhaps you were abused. Imagine the events which harmed you. Look them squarely and without flinching. This may take time to do and it will be painful. You may find yourself weeping inconsolably. Over time, as you cease pushing these things away, they will grow weaker. You may visualize them differently each time you imagine them. In this way you grow stronger and the power of what you were ruled by will diminish.

5. Perhaps you have no specific trauma but you have anxiety. This process works the same. You may be concerned about some event that is going to happen. Or perhaps you are worried about something which may happen, but over which you have no control. Ask yourself, what is the worst that could happen if this thing transpired?

One thing that is recommended by stoic philosophers is to imagine bad things happening so that we may prepare ourselves for their eventuality. For example, if you imagine the possibility of losing your job you might appreciate the employment more. If you routinely imagine that each work day might be your last, your perspective on your work situation may change. Things that troubled you may trouble you less as you realize that it could be much worse. You could have no means to support yourself or your family.

Yet there is a part of this visualization that is often missing. Your mind is able to adapt to many situations. When you imagine yourself losing your job, do you stop and then say to yourself that you are lucky to have the job? I recommend that you go further. Do not stop there. When you imagine the worst things happening to you, it is then time to ask yourself, "What then?" Part of the strength that you may gain from exercising your mind in this way is that you may understand your resilience. As you visualize the worst thing happening, imagine what will happen after that. And then what will happen afterwards.

The purpose of this exercise is to keep your mind strong, nimble, and flexible. You may say to yourself that losing your job would be a very tragic and sad thing. Yet if you do not run from the image of this situation you may realize that you have options. You may realize that you are stronger and more durable than you had imagined. You may realize that you are hardworking and that you will apply yourself duly until you find other work or start your own business. You may realize that you can exist with far less luxury than you have now. You may further realize the degree of love you have in your family and the support on which you can depend. Chief among these is that you realize that you have strength and that you can withstand more than you had previously thought. This is possible when you prepare your mind and go beyond the bad event. Simply visualizing the bad event is not enough. We must not only value our families, our jobs, and our health, we must value ourselves and our ability to withstand the troubles which life will give to us.

6. Trials which occur in life are opportunities for growth and development. Usually when one is in the middle of a crisis this is hard to see. Over time we can look back and see that we have been given another opportunity for growth. If you are passed over for promotion at work, there will be an opportunity for anger and resentment. You may carry bitterness within you and plot revenge. You may try to change the place you work. Or you may accept that the place you work is corrupt and look for other employment. In recognizing and accepting what you can and cannot change there is strength.

You may blame those who have treated you poorly. You may see that though they are in power over you, they are weak. You may grow to pity them. You may feel power in accepting the situation and in not letting it trouble you. You may leave the situation for something better. All of these things are possible. Recognizing the futility in trying to change others is useful. It is not that one cannot change others, it is that one rarely does so by aiming to do so. In our actions we may influence and inspire. We may advise. Yet we may see that unless circumstances change, the others who we wish to change will not change. The act of our leaving a situation may be the change of circumstances that causes them to adjust their behavior. In this way our actions are for our own benefit, yet they have some outward effect. Yet it must be understood that they change because they see it is to their benefit. If you leave to better your situation you lessen your grief. It is a direct consequence of your acceptance of what you can and cannot change. How much better to spend your days without the anguish of trying to change things you cannot.

I submit to you that as your perspective grows, so will your anguish diminish. As you understand others more thoroughly it becomes less easy to hate them and dismiss them as evil. They may do evil deeds, but they are still human. What good will it do you to add to the evil of their deeds by carrying anger and hatred within you? It is your choice. Your mind will be perturbed by such thoughts. Your emotions will remain anxious and fearful.

If you are in a bad situation it is your duty to leave if at all possible. If you are unable, you must understand that it is not your fault that you are in such a position. If you are ruled by those you think are evil it is not you who created the evil. Therefore don't create more evil by blaming yourself. Hatred of yourself is a worse evil than they could put you through. Understand that you can only do so much. Leave when you can. Until you are able to leave, remove your ego from the situation as far as possible. Further, do not create more evil by hating the ones who rule over you. Remove your hatred of these people by way of understanding them. To understand them isn't to like them or to approve of what they are doing. It simply means to have a greater perspective than you had before. View them as you would a child who has misbehaved. Recognize that they are much the same as children. By doing so your emotional reactions and torment will diminish. In this way you grow stronger. In this way you ready yourself to leave the moment you are able. Through acceptance you see the futility of fighting a losing battle and look to spend your energy on more productive things. Through this practice your mind becomes stronger and you become wiser.

7. True strength resides and springs forth from your mind. Your emotions may be an untenable and impossible sea unless you have strength of mind. Through the strength of your mind you can accept and overcome many things. My strength of mind allowed me to spend many years away from those I love against my will. Forced to live in a different country than they, I faced incredible difficulty. Through acceptance of the difficult situation I made a reluctant peace. If daily you think over your situation and face it with an open heart and mind you may see it differently. An impossibility becomes a challenge. A difficulty becomes an opportunity to grow stronger than you were. When there is nothing you may do about your situation, you can writhe in your misery or find a way through it. Often, we must begin by writhing in the pain. Yet we must find perspective or we might never leave that darkness.

To find that perspective you must look within. There is something inside of you, something your mind was designed to see, something it yearns to find. In this way we are all made to meet our troubles. We have strength to look at the pain and feel the pain. We have strength to absorb and move with the pain until it is part of our very framework. Having taken this pain into ourselves we become one with it and it ceases to be something we push against. It ceases to be something we run from. It becomes part of us.

In this way we may accept things and understand what it means to change our perspective on that which we may not change. In this way all things are possible, as all things are changeable.

Change is the constant in life. It is the sea upon which we find ourselves daily. Ask yourself when you wake each day what events you might meet with. In your ordinary day there are many things you might expect and some which you could never plan for. Contemplate your part in the universe and commit to the thought, "whatever happens to me, I will move forth with it to my best ability." There is no man who can boast that he has never been troubled. If you meet such a man do not trust his assertion. Recognize that he is lying to himself and presents that same fiction to you. Many are brave through the props of their ignorance of self. When you meet a man who tells you of his wrongs, his errors, his mistakes, and how little he knows, listen to him. If a man advises you and acknowledges that his understanding came from his own faults and mistakes, listen to him. I warrant that my understanding comes from committing more errors that I can recall. Yet it comes also from my acceptance of and learning from them. Stoicism is not a way of avoiding pain and troubles. It is a way of meeting them head on and accepting that life is filled with such things. In this way the things which once troubled you cease to trouble you.

8. Within your mind lies reason. It is available to you at all times, yet you may not be familiar with it. The same goes with virtue, which the ancient stoics have correctly called 'right reason'. When you encounter something that perturbs you, ask yourself why it perturbs you. What is it about this thing that causes me anxiety or anger? Perhaps it is the words of a parent, friend, or coworker. Perhaps it is some assignment at your work which you do not wish to carry out. Perhaps someone wishes you to meet with them or help them with such and such thing and you don't wish to be involved. Dig deep to the root of the thing and shine your reason on it. Perhaps you feel guilt or obligation to do the thing. Your impulse will be to run or to blame he that asked the thing of you. Yet if you look closely and stop your running and fretting about you may see that it is you who creates the obligation. It is you who makes yourself feel the guilt at wanting no part of it. In this way you create a second wrong to go with the first request. Even if he is in error in asking you to do the thing, or if he was not clear in his asking so that some confusion was created, you are better served to leave the mistake and error with him. Your mind can distinguish these two things and when you have uncovered them you have the opportunity to correct yourself. In this way you may set down your burden. In letting go of this burden you embrace your reason and in doing so adhere to virtue. The essence of this is being reasonable.

If someone angers you, you should feel the anger to its fullest extent. Do not believe those who will tell you that you should never be angry. To try and hold down your anger will only exhaust you to the point where you are too weak to control yourself—at this point the anger will have its day and you may be unable to stop yourself from doing something you regret. To be angry does not necessarily mean to give in to violence. It means that your mind has perceived the thing and has recognized the thing. If this thing cause you anger, feel the anger. Wear the anger on you for a time until it has evaporated. If possible keep your mouth shut and hold your tongue in the presence of others, unless you have some reason to let your anger out into the world. In keeping these things to yourself they do not grow as they would if you spread them to others. And indeed they may be a burden to others even if you give them this burden without meaning to.

9. The actions we take when angry and intent on getting revenge are seeds of some future outcome. In the same way, actions we take when filled with a peaceful feeling and intent on doing some helpful thing are seeds. In both cases we start something. In both cases there is some result. In both cases the thing we begin spreads farther than we could have imagined. It is our duty to use our mind to see how our actions might grow lives of their own. Do you imagine some violent revenge against someone? Can you see the future after that action? Do you see his widow and weeping children? Do you see yourself in prison, your wife and children also weeping? Do you see how the pain and suffering you create grow beyond the hateful moment? Any revenge you may succeed in attaining will be over in an instant, evaporated and followed by the cold realities which you created out of your anger. If you use your mind to visualize such things you recognize their futility and the ultimate evil that you would give rise to.

In this way your mind is your guide and may foresee much trouble before it has the opportunity to hatch from its planting. As humans we are blessed with this faculty, yet so many disregard it and abuse it. If we were mere animals we would have no opportunity to think through our possible actions and see their ultimate ends. Our ability to feel regret by simply thinking through a possible outcome keeps us from many a tragic mistake.

Yet, not all actions have such obvious good or bad outcomes. It is the grey areas of life in which we most need our stoic strength of mind. Our minds must be honed so that they can distinguish right from wrong when at first glance the outcome seems to be neither. When there is no obvious choice to be made we must do our best and accept the consequences honestly and without rationalization. If we find ourselves rationalizing we must own up to our error and move forward without much production. To be unfailing is impossible. To own up to our failings is possible, even if not always done.

10. The mind is the most flexible and useful tool we have. Adaptable to any situation, any problem, any grief. The greatest quality our mind may have is honesty. To see ourselves clearly, to see others clearly, and to see our reality clearly, these are our goals. It is in seeing ourselves clearly that we become aware of what we are able to achieve, what our faults are, and what our strengths are. To see others clearly is to see them as human beings, including their faults and weaknesses. In doing so we no longer consider them evil, nor do we consider them objects. In this way we may deal with other men fairly. And finally, in seeing our reality clearly we may understand what we may change and what we may not. This awareness is chief in our goals. The clarity of mind which makes this possible is our goal. By daily asking ourselves honest questions and not settling until we find honest answers is the way in which we achieve it. Learning from and then moving past our many failures is our duty.

11. Each day you should endeavor to read something which will enrich you. Whether philosophy, history, or something of the arts or sciences, make some time to sharpen your mind. Invigorate yourself by steeping your mind in the efforts of others who have come before you and toiled for your benefit. It is safe to say that there is not enough time to read all that one may hope to read. Yet, there is wisdom also in finding some few key works to which you return often. When something speaks to you and nourishes your mind, do not let it gather dust. As with a good friend, visit as often as is possible that you are enriched, yet, do not wear the company thin.

BOOK FOUR: REGARDING THE SPIRIT

1. Some say that there is little joy in a stoic life. To those I would reply: you may not know what a stoic life is made of. For is not contentment a primary fixture of such a life? The act of appreciating each moment for what it is; the actions of a stoic man undertaken to remain ethical and upright, these are things of joy indeed. Alongside your body and mind you must have spirit, which is the energy that runs through you. This energy you carry with you into every act. It is a posture of living, a stance, and a spring which remains at the ready for your use. Even in one's confusion and pain there can be found solace. It may bring some comfort to recognize that all who have come before you and all who will come after you will suffer the same things. For in this realization you may see that you are not alone. You're not the first to suffer these things, nor will you be the last.

No man can remain in a happy and positive spirit at all times. To attempt to be so would be foolish. It is not a matter of remaining happy and positive. It is not a matter of fooling oneself into believing the world is something which it is not. Nor is it a matter of fooling yourself into believing that you are something that you're not. It is from seeing the world, and yourself, as you are that your joy may come. The unending spring of joy and wisdom is at hand, though you may not see it. As Jesus said in the esoteric Gospel of Thomas, "the kingdom of the Father is spread out upon the earth, and men do not see it." The joy of your life is ever at hand, yet you may not see it.

2. Removing the obstacle to this joy is accomplished through unflinching acceptance of what is, while at the same time committing yourself to the leading of a better life. A life of ethics and reason is the good life. True joy in this life doesn't reside in riches, nor fame, nor praise from other men. True joy of spirit comes from applying yourself in each moment to working hard and from adhering to

principles. To falter and make mistakes need not diminish our joy, for we must understand that we are human and bound to fail. A generous spirit, both to ourselves and others, is what allows us to get up and carry on after mistakes and defeats. In the same way, our family and our fellow men may help us through their generosity of spirit. By bestowing on us their support and forgiveness may we rise and try again.

3. In kindness to ourselves and others is the wellspring of our joy. In greeting the morning with the acceptance that we will rise and work hard each day. In welcoming our rest when it is time to rest and enjoying the body's restorative benefits. In spreading good will to others through your actions. In sharing what you know with those who ask you and who may benefit from your perspective. In showing compassion to those who need our lenience and in standing firm to those who need our resilience and guidance.

In our pain and in our happiness there lies everything that is human about us. To neglect any part of ourselves is to do harm. Each day we may do some harm without knowing it, so we must be vigilant to ask ourselves what it is in us that requires care and attention. Just the same as we must ask ourselves if a plant needs more water, or more sun, or some fertilizer, so must we inquire about ourselves. As we would care for a child or a parent, so must we care for ourselves. As we would care for some new luxury item or device, so we must care for ourselves.

4. In a gentle and joyous spirit go forward and spread your goodness throughout the world. It is not necessary to preach to others, nor to make a show of oneself. In fact, these will only serve to distract from your goodness. Indeed they may detract from it. Spread your spirit through what you do as much as your words. Keep your words sparing and to good effect. As Seneca says, "we do not need many words, but, rather, effective words."

BOOK FIVE: REGARDING THE LIVING OF LIFE

1. The preliminaries have been addressed. From here I continue and speak to you as I speak to myself, for I need reminding of the good way of life. At times I may be tempted to stray from what is good towards what ails me, so I must refocus. At times I falter, and fail. Often I have looked back on my failures and shortcomings. It is through my own failures and mistakes that I have learned the most. There may be no other way.

Today there are many distractions pushing us and pulling us. We focus on tiny screens more than we do our fellow humans. We check our tiny accounts and leave the larger accounts in front of us untended. This is foolish. Our lives are around us and in front of us. They do not, on the whole, exist on these screens yet we often behave as if it were so. Though these devices may serve some purpose to us we should be careful how much energy we put to them. Make effort to rid yourself of the distractions which you do not truly need. Some may benefit you more than others and it is your task to understand which are beneficial and which are not. You may be surprised when you see how hollow a thing is, after truly looking at it.

2. Give your family and your friends your attention. Give them your energy. Put your spirit into your work and understand that you are on this earth to work. If you consider unending luxuries and pleasures to be your end game, if you seek to reside in sloth and count your money, you will find yourself off the mark. No one who embraces those paths will reach his full potential until he puts those ways down, for he will have resigned himself to beastly living. However gilded he may be, however much he has, if he doesn't know what is truly important, he remains a beast.

To your wife, give your best. To your husband, give your best. Your children are your priority, as are your parents. Your friends are your priority. If there be anything they need, see if there is something you might do to assist. Yet do not overwork yourself that you may appear busy and garner praise. When others are better served by helping themselves your action should be to allow them to do so. Stay out of the way when you are not needed so that others may achieve and learn.

Do not neglect yourself, above all other things. When you need exercise, take your exercise. When you need rest, take your rest. When your rest is done, be active and to the purpose. Use your time wisely and to the purpose. The purpose is to live and to live well, to live the good life. Your reward doesn't come tomorrow, or the next day. It will not come in the form of riches and if you seek it there you will find comforts, but not the good life. The reward is always present in the living of life now, in this moment, which is all that we have access to. As the ancient stoics have taught us: our past is lost and our future is unknown and uncertain. All we have is this moment and on the both sides of this moment are oceans of time which we may not enter. If your mind dwells in either of these oceans you will be tossed about on their waters and your vessel will be torn apart in the present. For no one can have more than one master. To be ruled by the past or the future is to leave the good life that is only possible in the present. By all means one must reflect on the past and plan for the future. But there is a difference between reflecting on the past or planning for the future and dwelling in the past or the future.

3. Some would say that stoicism is a philosophy embraced by life's losers—that they embrace it in order to dull the sting of their losses. While it is true that Epictetus, who was a slave until freed, embraced stoicism, it must also be remembered that Marcus Aurelius was a stoic. Easily the most powerful man on earth when he lived, his example demonstrates emphatically that the stoic way of life is a choice. Stoicism can be embraced by men who have great power, as well as men who are slaves. And let us not kid ourselves: many of us are slaves of one sort or another. Even those who have a modicum of success in our age are ultimately slaves even if they do not see it. Yet, within whatever slavery we are bound, we may find freedom.

Whether you be rich or poor, in terms of material wealth, need not determine how satisfied or happy you are with life. It need not determine how content you are. Contentment and acceptance of your situation are the starting points of the good life. They are the place from which all good things spring. From this place you may move forward and make the changes you wish to see in your life. It might seem like a contradiction, to be content and yet seek change, but it is no different than seeking to stand when you are sitting. Or seeking to get water when you are thirsty. No man remains thirsty just to remain thirsty. He drinks. Though you be content and accept your thirst, drink to quench that thirst. What you drink, or how much, is up to you.

4. Take joy in doing without things. When you don't truly need a thing, but you feel discomfort without it, ask yourself what you are doing. Understand how you fret over the thing and then understand how it is of no real consequence if you have the thing or not. When you are going about your day and you are met with an unexpected difficulty, go with it and embrace it. When you expect to eat one thing, but are faced with eating another thing, eat it gladly and do without the thing you expected. When you feel your first pang of hunger, do not eat, but rather feel the hunger. How quickly you may realize that you were only thirsty, or that you just felt a bit bored. After eight hours you will begin to feel actual hunger, which is a different thing than these. If your mission is to lose some fat from your belly, which is a common goal, enjoy the lack of food for longer periods. Enjoy the lack of sweets and other sugars which you have consumed prior in great quantity. When you are unable to have a thing, take some time to have perspective rather than feeling anger or frustration. And if you do feel anger or frustration, then feel it fully and allow it to pass. Then move forward.

5. When you feel anger towards someone—perhaps they have wronged you—do not respond out of anger. You may feel the urge to write to them and tell them your mind. You may feel the urge to say hateful things. You may feel the urge to strike them or throw something at them. Hold your tongue and your fist. Write the thing which you wish to send to them, but do not send it. If after two days

have passed you still feel it worthwhile to send, then you may contemplate sending it. I wager that your anger will have passed and you will no longer feel that urge. Over time you will develop the habit of letting your anger simmer and evaporate. Letting anger dissipate before you take action is a cornerstone of wisdom and a happy life. Of course, some will say that there are times when action is required. They are correct. Yet too often people are confused about what constitutes an action that demands violent response and behave badly. Do not commit this error and drag yourself down.

6. To your wife be a good husband and to your husband be a good wife. A good husband will provide for his wife and she will provide in turn for him. At times you must be firm with one another while at other times you must be gentle. If you have children the same rule applies. If you give them too much leeway it will serve to spoil them. Yet, do not be too strict either, as this will lead to a brittle connection and will serve to push them away from you. Strive for the middle ground as you should in all things. Husband and wife are two sides of the same coin. That which goes for the husband, goes equally to the wife, but in different shades and different degrees.

Knowing how to behave at which time takes trial and error. Above all else, keep love in your heart for each other and remember that you are both human and prone to make mistakes. Those who enter into marriage imagining that their spouse will never fail them are in for disappointment. Expect them to fail and expect of yourself that you will forgive them. Do not take advantage of this kindness in them and neither allow your own kindness to be taken advantage of. Support one another and tend to one another's needs. Keep your life together simple and enjoy the quiet times you may have together as well as the exciting times. Keep your home simple but pleasing to you both. Make it a place you are happy to be in and to return to after being out in the world. Fill your home with love and memories.

If your wife does something to disappoint or anger you, or slights you, how long do you hold onto the feeling? At any moment you are capable of embracing your reason and letting the slight go. It's amazing really, how long one can hold onto a slight. And equally amazing how easily it can be let go. In this way we may manage these disruptions between our spouses and ourselves. As you practice letting the thing go—for after all we are only human—you may laugh to yourself because it no longer seems comprehensible that you would hold onto the slight for as long as you used to.

Do your best to shield your family from the troubles of life. Do not bring your work troubles home to them. If you suffer some injustice at work, do your best to smile and leave those troubles at the door when you return home. In this way you make your home an oasis. Though you may feel abused and as a slave at work, do not burden your family with this and allow them to live free of the trouble. You will find that if you follow this practice, the troubles which seem so real during the work day vanish when you reach home. Over time, they become less real at work. Embracing this way builds strength and character.

7. To friends be a patient listener. Dispense advice only when it is sought for and keep your advice short and to the point. Keep real friends. As Marcus Aurelius teaches us to avoid false friends, you must learn the difference. Good friends will not delight in your misfortune, but will feel the misfortune with you. They will help you when you are in need and will not kick you when you are down. They will help you find levity at the end of your pain. Be the kind of friend to them as you would want them to be to you. Embrace your time with friends with a warm heart and feeling as you do time spent with yourself. Be honest with your friends. If they ask for your opinion give it freely and honestly. You will know your true friends because you may speak frankly with them. Acknowledge to yourself that your friends will make mistakes and that you will forgive their mistakes. As with your family, do not take advantage of their kindness nor allow them to take advantage of yours.

8. In all things be modest and walk the middle path. When you commit an error acknowledge it and move forward. Do not spend hours or days lamenting your mistake. Nor should you spend enormous amounts of time lamenting bad fortune. Within every event that happens to you there is an opportunity for some learning and growth. Challenges present you an opportunity to rise to them. No matter what happens, given enough time and perspective you

may see clearly the path that brought you there and the path that leads away from it.

9. The greatest power you can wield is power over yourself. To be presented with a temptation and to resist it is honorable and powerful. In each moment you have choices and the powerful man exercises his choices wisely—he reigns in his desires and does not abuse others. When someone is at a disadvantage, do you abuse them? Do you take from them what you should leave in their hands? Treat each man and woman as if they are your brother or sister—or as your children—and you will have cause to treat them fairly and justly. But, you may say, this man is a fool and is certainly not my brother. He may very well be a fool, but in more ways than you know he is your brother, so treat him so. Be patient with him and do not abuse him. If you cannot tolerate him and cannot instruct him then remove yourself from his company. If you cannot remove yourself from his company then tolerate his company as best you can and do what you can to help him improve. After all, perhaps there are things you may learn from him. And further, remember that life is short and you will soon die and none of the things he does which trouble you will trouble you for very long.

10. To your parents be thankful, respectful, and dutiful. Even if they be bad parents, they are your parents and deserve your respect and care. When they are old do your best to care for them and to be patient with them, as they were patient with you when you were a child. In this way we become parents to our parents. They may equally become as a sister and brother to you. Cherish your time with them for as long as you are able. Expect them to fail you as they are human. Since you were born they have understood that you would commit errors and have loved you nonetheless. Return that love to them despite their failings.

11. Wisdom and understanding of people is not a panacea or time without trouble. Often it is the same as seeing your child plot to do something wrong. Perhaps you have forbidden your child to do something yet you observe how they plan to deceive you. It is the same with adults as you go through life. As you see men more clearly you will see their failings and their scheming. Do your best to treat

them as you would your own children, however much it may sadden you to see how they behave. You may even see such behavior in those you report to at work. Have pity on them for as they plot and scheme behind yours and other's backs, they cheapen and lessen themselves.

12. In life be as a long distance runner. For many years I was such a runner. I would put down mile after mile. The good that came of it was in learning to endure pain. This is still something that benefits me in all areas of my life. The ability to endure things is at the core of stoicism. To endure hardships, lack of food and material comforts, these are hallmarks of inner strength. To push one's limits, whether they be physical, emotional, or mental, is benefited by setting one's aims on endurance. As I would once reach the ninth mile of a ten mile run, I would feel pains and aches even through the endorphins, yet I would continue. So close to the end is no place to give up. Now, at the seventh hour without food I set my sights on the eighth hour when the day's fast will end and I may finally eat a second meal. In both these ways do I endure and push myself. I use up what I have and gain much more.

And in other ways you may endure. The job that troubles you— you may plan to leave yet may have trouble finding new work. Put up with it then as best you can until new work is found. The separation from your loved ones—find some peace in your situation and look forward to its end. For if there be circumstances keeping you apart which you may not overcome, you must endure and do so as cheerfully as possible. Your loved ones will be bolstered by your strength and comforted by your resolve. To complain bitterly helps no one. To endure with a smile as often as you are able to muster is the only solution. When your time apart is over, then you may rejoice and be reunited. The sorrow of your parting and separation will be mended and is mended daily by an accepting and glad disposition. A loving heart, both for your loved ones and for life itself, will get you through most any difficulty. This does not mean that the things which you endure will be easy. In time they may get easier, yet it is the glad spirit of perseverance and fortitude which will carry you forward.

13. Endeavor to be just and lenient in all things. Observe how various religions pit themselves against one another. Further observe how non-believers pit themselves against all believers. Do not make the beliefs of others, or the lack thereof, your concern or cause of ire. Be temperate and understand their needs. Yet do not allow them to abuse the leniency and harm others under the guise of piousness. Punish those who use force or threat to hoist their beliefs on others. In this way you will be as a prince among men—lenient and yet firm.

14. To your children pass on wisdom and the art of living well. What better gifts could you bestow on them? If you leave them riches, yet do not show them how to live well with or without riches, it will be like handing them a weapon. The weapon will be one which harms them over time. Teach them to love hard work and the application of their minds. Teach them to love learning and wisdom above all other things. Teach them to seek understanding of themselves and of the world. If you are satisfied that they have learned these things you may safely bestow your riches to them. They must understand that they are able to live a complete life with or without them. If they do not learn this they will be lost and none of your riches will help them.

Yet, do not be a miser as some have. One of wealthiest men of our age has left his children little at all. It seems that he has taken little steps to teach them how to live, but rather, has wished them good luck in the world that they should find their own way. In this way he has failed them on both counts and must be counted as a fool. To focus only on sparing a child one's riches is no better than to spare them your life's lessons. In both cases the child is disserved. Many men earn vast riches, yet it is rare to find one among them who knows how to shepherd his flock well and provide for them.

14. If you teach from darkness you will spread darkness and the darkness will grow and consume you. Be light, teach light, and spread your light in the world as seeds. Let your actions be good as often as you are able. Live well and let go when it is time to let go. When you realize the end is at hand, think to yourself, "At least there will be peace."

15. Be a lover more than a fighter. Yet, when you must fight to defend those you love: be ruthless. Remember that in those times there is no such thing as 'fighting'—there is only war. Make an absolute war against those enemies who would break with nature's law and harm your loved ones. Put them asunder. Remember that some men will view leniency and kindness as weaknesses to be exploited. Keep your eyes close on such men. Be wary of them as you will more often come across their type in life than you will those with wisdom and clarity. When you catch such a man in a lie, a deceit, or a ploy against you, do not let it go further. Let the punishment fit the crime.

When you stand on the right side of things you may often stand alone. Prepare for this and equip your mind for the possibility. You may lose much as you gain much.

16. Care less about what station a man holds and care more for how he inhabits his station. Often a man will have a high position and yet will keep the habits of a man below his station. I say below meaning one of low moral character. Be on the lookout, for many in high places lack morals and ethics. The world knows more darkness because of them, whatever their politics, because they hold power over others: decision-making powers, financial powers, and legal powers. I submit that the world would know more light if each man made more effort to embrace his reason and had a moral code. Lacking these ethics, human beings become as rats. Do not let yourself become a rat, no matter how high you ascend. The temptations to take off others' plates will grow tenfold, then a thousand fold, as you raise in the ranks of power. Keep a commitment to yourself that you will ever remain human and never allow yourself to fall so low. Though you be alone in a horde of a million rats, do not become a rat.

17. Practice self-control, restraint, and willpower. Though you may have some food in your kitchen which you desire, control your appetite. For you know that you have a diet to keep which will allow you to reach the fitness you desire. It may be easy to imagine the food, to picture yourself taking it, to predict how good it would taste if you put it in your mouth. Yet, while not as easy thus far, you may

also imagine yourself walking by the food, admiring it, and saving it for a later time. In picturing your self-restraint you cultivate an image of yourself which may not yet exist, but which you know is possible. Perhaps you are not fully convinced that you are strong enough? Very well then, you must learn this first. And with each small step you learn strength which was yesterday unknown to you. I tell you that your capacity for withstanding things is limitless, yet you must cultivate it day by day. It is easy, yet difficult.

18. Do not shy away from any kind of work. Particularly when young it is good to learn the different kinds of work which may be required in life. Learn to cook and bake bread; to sew and mend your clothes; to chop wood and build fires; to repair things; to plant, tend, and harvest crops; to take orders and give them well and without malice on either side; to make shelter outdoors with your bare hands; to trim trees and hedges; to lay mulch, cut grass, and rake leaves; to clean your home; to polish your shoes; to cut your own hair; to take an engine apart and put it back together; to weld and rivet; to sharpen your knives; to catch fish; to do basic plumbing; to change oil and brakes; to teach others; to make inquiries and investigate; to plan and build; to read and write letters; to invent; to shelve books; to push and lift heavy things; to work in a factory; to load things onto palettes and unload things from them; to drive; to sit and keep watch.

If there be any task required of you, do it cheerfully as you can and recognize the reward held in the increased knowledge of experience. Explore and learn what kind of work it is that you enjoy most—that which hardly seems like work at all.

19. Travel and see things with your own eyes, taste new foods, smell new smells, meet new people and learn their customs. Experience things first hand. Yet, do not spend your whole life in travel if it be an escape. Do not run from yourself. Travel until you know what you need to know and then return to that which you left from, even if it be in a different place. Your home is within you and once you have found it your constant journeying may come to an end. As Seneca reminds us, "Everywhere is nowhere".

20. Do not concern yourself with the popularity of others. Some

will fan their own flame. Others may grasp hold of a current trend. They quickly will make friends, enemies, fortunes, and fame. Does this bother you? Perhaps you feel a fire, a rush of inspiration to do better than them. Embrace this competitive spirit, but before you rush headlong into turmoil, ask yourself what is the matter? Why this urge to quell inferiority and what is the source of that inferiority? Conquer that question and you may hold an easy smile rather than envy.

Learn admiration instead, especially for those who promote and embody the qualities you value most. Find brothers along the same road rather than enemies against whom you must compete. Despite what some will teach you, it is not a zero sum game.

21. When you are faced with an important decision, and have the luxury of time, do not decide hastily. Resist the temptation to rush to judgment, rather, sit for a time with your options and weigh them carefully. One may be the clear favorite—very well then let it wait a little while for you to ponder. If it is the correct choice it will win no matter if you decide in five minutes or five days. If you have no such luxury of time then go with the option which your experience and your inner voice tell you. Be wary of making such decisions based on fear, as you may likely go astray. Therefore, be honest with yourself and lay out what reasons you have for each option that you may get to the bottom of your inclinations.

Importantly, once you make your decision stick to it. Unless circumstance truly warrant a change in position, hold firm. This is the reason to consider things carefully, that you may have no stone to be turned over later which will catch you by surprise. In this way may you be decisive and steadfast. Yet, do not continue over a cliff just because you have turned in its direction.

22. In choosing a wife, find a woman who has an inner beauty to match her outer beauty. Recognize that all outer shells will fade and that you have more than her looks to consider. Will she be a good mother to children? Will she care for you when you take ill? When you discuss important matters with her does she only seek her own benefit? Is she afraid of working diligently until the task is done?

Does she carry herself in a feminine and graceful way? Is she easy to smile and does she have a gentle touch? Does she have a kind and loving temperament? Does she also have a fighting spirit when needed? Is she skilled in the art of socializing with others when necessary? These are questions to ask yourself. Look deeper than her skin which will one day wrinkle, her hair which will one day turn to grey, and her breasts which may one day lose their composition. By all means, a husband and wife should find the other pleasing to look at but you should assign importance to how pleasing she will be to live with. Consider that for many years you may share a home. What will she be like in five, ten, or twenty years? How well will her demeanor wear over time?

23. A man doesn't need many friends, but good and loyal ones. May you pick those who are true, trustworthy, and loyal. If you tell everyone your business you will find that soon your private matters have spread much further than the ears who have heard it directly. A true and loyal friend will not discuss with others what you have told him in confidence. Treat your friends as you would wish to be treated and look for men who treat you accordingly.

24. How often have you been avoiding some necessary task? How often have you walked past it and said, "Tomorrow"? And how often have you said to yourself, "Very well, let's just get on with it"? How often have you felt better when your work is done, rather than having it hanging over your head for tomorrow? And how often have you decided to meet some task cheerfully and it turned out to be a much more pleasant experience and not the drudgery which you expected? This is a tool for the good life. Use it often.

25. What are you attracted to in people? Are you attracted to honesty, straightforwardness, and cheerfulness? Are looks or power more important? When you see a beautiful woman, peer beneath the surface. The qualities she possesses, the things which she values, all become apparent if you open your eyes and ears. Look closely and you may find a woman who has a constant spring of affection and honor within her heart. There will be few like this in your life.

It is the same with friends. Look into a man's eyes and listen to him talk. What does he concern himself with, what are his aspirations, and what does he hold in his heart? Look closely and you will know if he is a man who can be a trusted friend. There will be few like this in your life. In time you will realize that your hesitation to talk to some women stems from seeing what is beneath the surface. Experience will have taught you to recognize which fruit is ripe—if you eat the wrong fruit it is sour, bitter, and you must spit it out. Gather the ripe fruit into your life.

26. Many of us will find ourselves in jobs that we do not like. When we started out at the job things were different: we had hope, things were new and fresh, and we felt certain we were at a good place. And then things changed. Either the organization changed, or we changed. In either event we find ourselves in a new situation and desire to leave. Perhaps the organization has become corrupted; perhaps new management has come in and has destroyed the moral of the company; perhaps people have been put in positions not because they are the most qualified but because they are on the best terms with the manager. These are all things which we may face and which cause us to fret and become disgusted with our jobs.

These situations are not easy. Hardly any of us has the means to just walk away and at present it may not be easy to find a new job. Perhaps you are older and over-qualified. Perhaps you are younger and under-qualified. Regardless of the specifics you may find that for some period you must continue working at the job you have come to loathe. I tell you that in this loathing lies the greater part of your misery. Endeavor to find something good about your situation. Do not pretend that the bad isn't there, do go ahead and acknowledge it: don't pick up a grenade and pretend it's a flower.

Yet you must acknowledge that things could be worse: you could have no job and no means to support yourself or your family. And you must further acknowledge that the anger and resentment which you carry towards that envied co-worker, or the incompetent boss, only serve to hurt you more. While they commit the wrong, you carry another wrong deep in your heart which weighs you down. Realize that you cannot change the situation, that you cannot change the people and the organization, that you may only change yourself. This doesn't mean that you should suddenly decide that everything is okay, it means you should make your peace with it, for your own sake. And then do everything you can to find something better.

27. Do not avoid things. Realize how much trouble you cause yourself when you avoid something which you imagine to be painful, dull, or laborious. Is there someone at work who you don't like to run into? Do you try and time your trips away from your desk so you do not see them? Recognize how you chain yourself and erode your freedom. Visualize yourself in the situation. Imagine running into them. What is the worst that can happen? Even if you despise this person, even if they are your boss and an imbecile, do your best to be cordial to them and do not avoid them. You do not need to make glad hands with them or be saccharine. But it behooves you to stop avoiding them. The same applies to many things in life. Meet the things you avoid head on and you will free yourself and end those troubles which you've created by avoiding them in the first place.

28. Has your life not turned out as you had intended, hoped for, and planned for? There is no way to foresee what will happen in the course of our lives. We may plan for years for some eventuality only to find that it has become impossible. Imagine those who have worked hard for many years only to have their retirement savings taken from them by crooked men. This is but one recent example. Imagine those who work diligently at their studies only to find that there are no jobs for them as they'd imagined would be. Even those with advanced degrees find that things have contracted so much that they have few options. Do you find yourself in such a position? Perhaps you find yourself stuck in a dead-end job with no hope for another. Perhaps you apply for countless positions and either hear nothing or are rejected. These are all commonplace for us today and present great difficulty to our spirits. How easy it is to become jaded, cynical, and to blame the world or oneself. Yet we must resist this temptation and understand that we are but one person in a large and complicated world. How much control over your destiny do you have, really? If you're honest you'll realize that you have far less power to change things than you thought. You may apply yourself diligently for years and have nothing to show for it. Then, by some chance meeting with a friend who has some connection, find that

opportunities have suddenly opened for you. These opportunities never existed before and you could not have imagined them being open to you. Then you may look back at the intervening time and realize how much of it you wasted in bitterness and feelings of self-loathing and defeat. Why ruin your life the more? If you do your best and still do not win the day, what reason have you to moan and beat yourself? You have no such reason and can only blame yourself if you ruin the time you have in such ways. Life is short and much of it is beyond our reach. We must do the best we can with what we have and not make ourselves slaves by wishing for what we cannot have, nor by moaning and cursing ourselves or others for what we cannot have.

29. Time and time again I've found myself looking outside myself for something to complete me. After struggling until I am weary, I return inwards, to the fountain that has always been there and drink. I seem to know the whole time I am wandering that I am astray, yet, when I return I am welcomed as a son. Remember that you only waste your time and energy in seeking outside yourself which only lies within.

30. Do not place too much value on your possessions, for they are just things. Do not horde them away, nor keep some for special occasions only. If you have a thing, use a thing. If you have no use for it, find some better home for it where it may be used. Take care of the things you have and do your best to keep them in the best working order possible. Of all your possessions, value those which elevate you most and expand your understanding.

Rather than valuing possessions, value the people in your life. Your family firstly, then your friends, and all other social connections afterwards. Treat all men you meet as your brothers and all women you meet as your sisters.

31. For those who are in the military, law enforcement, judiciary, and public office; for anyone who may come to have vast power over others: take special care with the powers which are entrusted to you. Do not abuse others with this power as you will debase yourself as much as you debase them. If you act harshly and punitively, without

true provocation of such action, you will create enemies who will do much to achieve your destruction. Why would you do such a thing? What need have you to abuse others? And for those in the position to give orders to those below, consider well and fully what you require and demand of them. If you hold their fate in your hand you will be asking much of them to refuse those orders if they be immoral and lacking ethics. Save everyone the trouble you would create and be a moral and ethical man. Do not bring shame upon yourself, your family, your community, or your country by acting tyrannically.

Embrace fairness with all who you encounter. Do not wish rashly for harsh punishments for others, rather wish for their reform and do your best to assist in that reform. Harsh punishments are sometimes necessary, but there is often more distance between the present and that eventuality than many would acknowledge. Apply sound judgment. Take time to consider thoroughly each situation which you encounter. Be lenient when leniency is required, yet be fair and implacable to those who would abuse and take advantage of others.

For those who have stolen vast fortunes from the many you should treat them thusly: seize their possessions. Imprison them and their families. The condition of their release will be in returning those ill-gotten gains, even those which have been stored abroad. Remove all credentials they may have required, and all licenses so that they may not practice their evil again. Forgive all debts which may have been accrued to them and release any who may be bound to them by contract. Let them live in poverty and strike down any chance they may have at regaining their footing. In essence, humble them in every way, save taking their lives.

And to our military, those who have fought valiantly and have trained to protect us from dangers lurking without—know that we depend on you to protect us equally from dangers lurking within. Hiding in plain sight are those who would abuse us and destroy us. Those who control the very means which we use to sustain ourselves. Those who lie and manipulate and deceive us. Those who profit from thin air. There may come a time when you must take up arms against them and restore what has been stolen and perverted by their greed and hypocrisy. Do not worry about those who would say you commit some error, for they only do so to discourage you from displacing them. You must remember that you are protecting those who are defenseless, and that you also protect your own. For how many of your men and women have been sent to their own deaths and destruction, or to cause that of others, by greedy and immoral men? How many more will? Unless you displace them, they will continue to abuse and displace you as well as us. Very well then, take up arms against them and be done with half measures. Restore what's golden and remove what is rotten.

32. Remain rational amid the screeching of the crowd. Are there those who we are not supposed to criticize or make fun of? Indeed, and there are harsh penalties for making light of them. Remember that this is an evil and that you should not further it, but instead should counter it.

Recognize that you have been conditioned for a long time to behave in what is called a 'politically correct' way. At the very mention of these groups we have been conditioned to bristle and feel discomfort lest anyone criticize them. At the very criticism of these groups, or even the satire of them, we have been conditioned to brand the critic as a heretic against society. Disregard this and embrace your reason. Keep a light and stalwart heart. Challenge those who would hold their madness up to you and kick against it.

33. You are a part of nature. Though you appear to be a discrete being, you are in fact connected to all that is outside of you. In truth there is no outside, only the appearance of such. For when you breathe, your body makes use of the air, consumes it, and makes the air part of your body. And when you exhale you give back something to the air, though it has been changed. This process is continual and includes your skin and all other stimuli which you may perceive.

Therefore, when you see an ill committed, do not create another ill inside of yourself. As much as is possible turn this ill to good with your understanding and lenity. If you must be firm and steadfast against the ill then do so with all your being.

If someone is rude to you, feel the sting of it, and let it go as quickly as possible. This is an aim. You may not be able to adhere to this aim at all times, and if you are unable to not fret and worry. Simply do your best and aim to do better next time. Neither should you become slack in your efforts to live via reason and virtue. But, do not be too harsh either.

34. When your child makes a mistake, do not automatically punish them harshly. Be lenient and full of love for the child. If they disobey you and disrespect you then you must punish them and make sure that they understand what is happening. They must learn one way or the other how to live and to honor their parents. Correct their error so that they may learn, yet not learn to hate you. Be firm so that they may not take advantage of your kindness. They should love and respect you, doing everything in their power to please you and live up to your expectations. When your children are thus you will know you are taking care of them properly. Encourage them to do their best. Make sure that they know what they are capable of and what they should strive for. Expect them to fail you and in this expectation you will not meet their error with a huge disappointment, but rather, you will meet it with the loving consolation and correction of a good father.

35. In order for the world to become better, every person must endeavor to live by a code of ethics. Some are in a position to do more good for more people and the burden rests on their shoulders to do so. Do they respond? If those who have trillions of dollars of wealth were to behave differently, think of how the world might be better. And yet, in your own way, from day to day and moment to moment, you may make your world better by acting differently. Simply treat others fairly, as you would want to be treated. It's simple advice which is often given, yet it is true.

And we should keep in mind that it may be easy enough for us to avoid certain temptations and to live the good life in our present circumstances. But how would we respond if things were different? Imagine that someone approaches you and offers to clear all of your debts, to clear any legal misgivings you may have done from your record, to pay off your house or buy you a new one, to award you with a salary you could never have previously imagined. For this, you are required to do their bidding with no questions ask. And what if their commands would lead you to do evil? This is the proverbial deal with the devil and many have accepted it. Would you? Would you be able to refuse it? It is hard to imagine being able to do so, but it is possible. And I say to you that if the world is to be bettered you must. The only exception being if you are able to influence those who have resources and do great evils. If you could teach them to behave differently you might very well save lives. But this is all rather dubious isn't it? For in general the men who have that wealth and power are not moral men and did not gain that wealth through moral means. Rather, they acquired it through deceit and violence upon others. Very well then, perhaps violence towards them is what must come. If it can be avoided all the better, but we do not live in a perfect world.

36. In all things embrace fairness and justness. Embrace patience and leniency. Embrace reason and sound judgment. Allow others their dignity.

37. Be ever wary of deceit and those who would deceive you. Be ever wary of your own comfort, of what leads you to it, and keeps you there. Keep your mind sharp and ask yourself difficult questions. Do not shy away from their answers. As though you are coming close to a steep cliff: your natural impulse is to stay away, yet you must approach it and peer down to see what is there. The world is filled with darkness. Do not allow this darkness into your heart and mind. Rather, be a beacon and allow your light to exist within you and around you.

38. In dealing with regret, the first thing is to recognize that you are but a man and bound to have failures. Whether this is from lack of action or wrong action, the feeling of regret may sting you. Yet ask yourself: Did the great men of the ages never make mistakes? Did Verus not fail to send Marcus Aurelius to the armies to experience battle and soldering? Certainly he left his adopted son and later emperor ill-equipped for what laid ahead of him. Did Marcus himself never err? These great men of the ages, pick one it doesn't matter who, have all had a hand in some failure of action or inaction. Do

you expect more of yourself? To raise such a bar and hold yourself to it is too cruel. You must be lenient and forgiving of yourself—that is the first thing. And of course you should expect failures from those you love most. Deal with them with leniency and forgiveness.

But this is only the first step, the acceptance. To look coldly on your error and not to wince. For if you look away, you are likely to stumble on it once again. This won't do. So, having looked at yourself squarely, you must commit yourself to learning from the mistake. You must commit to doing better at your next opportunity. Yet be mindful of the fact that you may trip up again. Maybe not as wholly, maybe in a different way, but it may happen nonetheless. Do not despair if this happens, but remember what I have told you. You are no different than the great men of the ages in your errors. However, to distinguish yourself you must stay vigilant and honest in your endeavors to remain upright and true. With each few steps forward you take, you may fall down. Rise again and take a moment to reflect, then carry on. Life is such.

39. Keep watch over yourself. Notice how you tend to certain quick tempers. Do you grow impatient easily with those you love? Do you find yourself giving in to some habit of temper? Realize that you may at once dispatch this habit and mood. Free yourself immediately from its bonds as you do not need such slavery. In a moment you may set down that mood and embrace a new one. Do not believe, falsely, that because a mood has started you must finish it out to the end. How foolish a way of life that is. Must you finish every bit of food that is set before you? Must you drink all that comes before you? Nonsense. You are not bound to do that and neither are you bound to complete and carry out a feeling just because it has come on you. Feelings come and go as do the breeze which cools you or makes you sweat. How powerful to realize we are not bound to our moods as we are the winds around us. Nature sends one, we command the other. Do not be a slave to things which you are master.

40. You may come to a dark place where the road seems at an end. No one can ask you to continue when there is no reason to do so. Yet, have you exhausted all of the options? Can you really say you

have searched your reason for all its solutions and responses? Know that life will present you with challenges. Those you hold most dear, they who you love most may at times seem to be at cross-purposes. They may in fact seem to seek your destruction. But is this so? Have you considered that they may be striving for answers as well and have come to some painful and emotional conclusions? Remember to embrace your reason and take two steps back to look at things clearly. Reign in your automatic responses to their actions. Take care that you not throw away what is good because you have seen its darker side. Do not all objects cast a shadow?

41. When you find you cannot sleep, do not lay in the bed for hours moaning or trying to sleep. If your body will not fall into sleep then get up and make use of the time. Perhaps your body is weary but your mind is active. Perhaps you took coffee or tea and your mind bursts with ideas. Write them down. Or perhaps you have nervous energy. Find something worthwhile to do with your time. Read, clean, sharpen your knives—whatever it is that needs doing, do it with a glad and welcome heart.

42. How easy it is to have a dark and hardened temper towards others. In the crowded street when you want to pass, you'll find two or three people walking side by side, and slowly at that. You may have the urge to exchange words with them or to shove them. Hold yourself. Pass as you may, but why engage them any further? Will it change them? It is impossible to know the reason why they walk as they do and take up the space for passing. Acknowledge your frustration but do not take it out on them. There is no doubt that they are annoying, but have you not also been so?

43. Go with the ebbs and flows of life. Do not fight your own current, for it is taking you where you were always meant to go.

44. Remain prepared for the unexpected, for it will always arise. Learn to greet it cheerfully or at least cordially. To be disrespectful to the things that arise from Nature's course is to disrespect yourself and all the possibilities that unexpected events present to you.

45. Do not spend all waking hours in pursuit of pleasures, nor

riches, nor comforts. Rather than thinking of this way of life as denial of self, think of it as a way to realize and develop your true self, the self that is but a potential now. In the same way that you should not shrink from hard work, do not shrink from developing your potential in favor of fulfilling the transient and unquenchable needs of your ego. Learn to appreciate your undeveloped potential as you would a young child.

46. If you eat poison every day do not be surprised when you get sick. Be wary of what you consume, both in content and quantity. The company you keep, the things you read and watch, all become part of what you are and influence you for better or worse. Some things may be beneficial in small doses but troubling or even deadly in greater ones. Other things may have no effect unless consumed in great quantities.

47. Look around you. Everywhere you turn you are bombarded by images, sounds, lights—advertising is relentless. Do you realize the effect it has on you? Do you realize that if you see the same brand image a hundred or a thousand times, you are more likely to select that brand when it is presented to you against a rival? Familiarity with that brand image is powerful. And yet, consider that you are not only being bombarded with brand images, you are also being bombarded by images of certain realities. That is to say, certain types of reality are being shoved in front of you, day in and day out. Do you realize the effect this has on you? Are you willing to go against the grain of your conditioning when you are presented with a rival?

Consider that it behooves some to convince you to behave one way rather than another. Yet, is that way in your own best interest? Is it in the best interest of your family, or your country? You must prepare your mind daily to be aware of what is being thrown at you. Like a shield your mind must remain vigilant to guard against unwelcome messages. If you wish to remain chaste, understand that there are many images put in front of you encouraging you to end your chastity. And so on. Hold onto your center and your ideal of what you most value and consider at all moments if you are behaving according to your virtue or according to some conditioning.

48. If you chase after a thing to exclusion of all other things, you may eventually attain it. What will you do then? Will the thrill of the chase be over leading you to abandon the thing you strove so hard to get? Imagine in your mind what life would be like with the thing (the job, love conquest, new car or electronic toy) and dig deep into what that thing holds for you. Do you really need or desire it once you've meditated on it thusly? If so, by all means go forward and achieve it. The thing is to know what you're doing. But, you may say, what about following my passion and lust for life? Very well then, I am not a tiresome schoolmaster. Go ahead and enjoy the thrill of life. I do not judge or suggest that you not enjoy the moment. A quick decision to go to some new thing and enjoy something never enjoyed is one thing—abandoning your life in the mindless pursuit of something you do not actually need is entirely different. My aim is to guide you so that you look two steps ahead of yourself before you commit fully to a mistake you may not recover from.

49. Focus on the simple things of life. Each small action, every tiny moment, these are the things to care for and pay attention to. When you do a thing, do it deliberately and with concentration. How often have I seen men doing work, that many would feel is beneath them, with enthusiasm, a smile, and a glad heart. How much happier and content they are with life than those who spend their hours worrying over vast fortunes and how to spend the interest they have gained in the last several hours. Imagine if they too had the focus and enthusiasm of the common workers I have seen, oh what lives they might live. The joy they might spread to others with their fortunes. Such men do exist but they are rare. Endeavor to be such a citizen of the world, regardless of your social status. If you are a president or chancellor, be the best that you can be. If you are a garbage collector, be the best that you can be. Wherever you are, perform your duties with a glad heart. Better your situation as you may and remember the principles that will ground you in a good life.

50. Be as good to others as you would have them be to you. As Marcus Aurelius teaches: if a thing is good, do it; if a thing is not good, do not do it. In every moment we have the opportunity to do good or ill. We have the opportunity to admonish those who do ill or to be lenient and understanding when they have observed their own

ill. We always have room to improve our responses, as we always have room to improve our actions and decision making. Do not rush forward into things when you are not certain. If more time is needed, take as much time as is required. Weigh all of the facts. Ignore speculation unless it comes from a trusted source. Be wary of your own speculation and root out its causes. Whenever your mind is troubled and restless, take a moment to sit and reflect. What haunts you? Where are you being driven and why? If you let the storm pass you may find there is no need to rush to a thing or away from a thing. Then you may rest comfortably in the present and embrace all it has to offer you. In this way we may be healed of the injuries we have suffered since childhood. We didn't know how we were set on a course to run and hide from ghosts and monsters which haunted us then. Perhaps we were ill-used or neglected. Perhaps we've been running to find some nourishment or to escape some harm. Yet those things are in our past and have been internalized. It is up to us now to look inward and see them, to acknowledge them, to embrace them, to shake their hand, to place a blanket on them when they are cold, and then to step forward out of their shadow. To live. To grow. To love all that we are meant to love and reward all that we are meant to reward. Keep your heart light with the knowledge that there is nothing you need do to find your light except embrace that which you are. It is in running from that light that you found and embraced darkness. Darkness is no more real than light. Choose that which allows you to see clearly.

51. Many are consumed with thoughts of revolution. Yet, the first revolution must take place within yourself. Can you say you have cleaned your own house well enough to tell others how they should clean theirs? Is your mind clear? The second revolution must take place at home, with your family. Keep everything well for them and see to their needs. Once these are taken care of properly, then you may think of other revolutions. Begin with every interaction with other men throughout your day. Master this and you will be ready to master other things, but not until then.

52. Remember how much you have to learn, though you may have learned much. Let it always be your approach and outlook on life that you should take a step back and learn from the moment. Assume you

have not learned enough, though you may be wise. Keep the words of wise men with you and meditate on them daily. Begin each day with contemplation and thoughts over what good you may do that day.

53. In your relationships you may be accused of being cold, aloof, or unfeeling. Do not react harshly to such criticisms and understand that your loved ones are giving you their honest perspectives. To them you may in fact seem cold and aloof. Do not reproach them or admonish them harshly. Reassure them of your tender feelings towards them and wait for another moment to instruct them as to your beliefs. Or, if you do instruct in that moment of their vulnerability, do it kindly and do not be long-winded. Once they have absorbed the lesson put down the teaching and make this your habit in general. Belaboring the point will not behoove either of you and may serve to turn them away, considering you pedantic.

Even as you maintain your equilibrium and state of mind you must meet your loved ones at the gates of your serenity. If you ever remain inward, what profit can come to them from your presence? Serve them and come out of your shell if it means serving them well. If you want to be a good husband, let the peace and harmony you feel come through in your actions and words to your family. When conflict arises be the steady dock onto which your family may tether themselves, lest they fall into harsh waters. Even as you lose yourself you must be strong and regain your footing—for your own sake as well as theirs.

54. How corrupt we are, how easily we forget ourselves and our patience. It is for this reason that we write such things and read philosophy. For what man can walk the straight path at all times without guidance and reminders? I wager there are few. Therefore, let each day be a practice and remembrance. Take care each morning to remind yourself of the things you have forgotten the day before. Your life is fragile. Every moment you spend with your loved ones might be your last. This seems incomprehensible when we've lost our patience with one another so let us be mindful of the fact before we utter harsh words. How often I have let my temper slip towards those I love, so I must meditate on this especially and humble myself

in front of my ignorance. No man is above learning what he needs to learn, though he may think otherwise.

55. Today I watch over myself. Today I look back over the week's mistakes. How easily I have gone astray and lost myself. I must be honest and look upon the mistakes clearly and logically. I could have done better. When I lost my temper with my loved ones, I could have done better. When my tempers flared at other situations—with complete strangers—I could have done better. Why have I worried so much over trivial things? Yet in the revisiting of these mistakes and failures I can find some leniency and forgiveness of myself so long as I endeavor to improve. And when would be a better time than today? The apple is ripe so I will cut into it and savor it. The orange is ready to be peeled. The bread has risen and the meat has cooked and rested. Feast then, on life, and return to the goodness of your inner nature. Be rational, be just, and be reasonable. If all men endeavored so, especially those who enjoy powerful rule, imagine how better the world would be. Imagine it and make it happen each day as much as possible in your own way. For virtuous living is its own reward. Religions will provide some rewards in heaven, but what if there is nothing more? Either way you should be virtuous and embrace your reason. This is the way to proceed and grow and live. Be rational, be just, and be reasonable.

56. Make peace with this moment. Be like the balloon, which, when let go of by the little child, rises and rises, until it has disappeared. Take in the scene. Observe the boats in the harbor; the children playing basketball below; the cable cars rising into the distance across the harbor until they reach the mountains on the other side, becoming tiny then invisible; the cars, taxis, double-decker buses, cement mixers, vans and trucks on the highway appearing, then disappearing; the people walking to the shops and rising in the glass elevators; the small boats on the waters gliding under the bridges and the wake they create; the large cranes unloading the shipping vessels; planes landing and taking off in succession, one after the other; the children walking hand in hand with their parents; the old walking slowly and deliberately, each step a triumph; the hawkers handing out cards and selling wares; the shopkeeper taking a break to have a cigarette; the butcher chopping the meat with blazing

speed on the special wood block made for that purpose and the blade as well; the baker and noodle maker; the pancake and waffle stand with the line down the block; the ferries, running every six minutes like clockwork and without fail; the streetlights and their sound as you may cross; the subway approaching with voice alerting you to mind the gap; the sound of the card being swiped to let you in and out of the subway; the young couples kissing on the bus; the tea shop, also with its long line; the fish market and sea smells; garbage rotting and cooking on the street; flowers in shops perfuming the air as you walk by; endless shops and wares for sale as you walk by; All of these things you should observe and take care to absorb and remember.

57. When I have something to say, writing is easy. It is when I want to say something, but do not have the words or know what it is that I wish to say, that writing is difficult. In life we should keep silent when we have nothing to say. So it should be when we have nothing to write. Be patient and let your mind turn over what life has shown you. When you have learned something new, write about it. Share when you have something to share; otherwise, keep silent.

58. When you are fatigued, you must rest. How often have you found yourself struggling against the tide, making yourself wearier by the moment? Nothing can benefit from this practice. Make a new habit of putting yourself in bed, or in chair, or couch. Close your eyes and let your mind wander. Allow it the space it needs to recuperate and become fertile again for ideas. You cannot plow a field constantly and expect crops. Why would you expect anything less from your mind?

59. At times you will put your thoughts forth as you would throw a pebble into a pond. On some occasions there seem to be no ripples. Yet, later you may see ripples as they move outward from your throw. Perhaps others have been influenced by your thought and have internalized and adopted it. Or perhaps they have the same thought. Or perhaps they were influenced by another. Yet do you find yourself wanting credit? It may never come and in fact it may not be deserved. Even if it is, do you really lose anything if you are not recognized? The good act is done, do you need more? Does the

sun ask for credit for shining each day? Does the good father always ask for praise or thanks from his children for being a good father?

60. The Greeks gave us more than Stoicism. Use vinegar to disinfect cutting boards, knives, counter tops, and even fruits and vegetables. Get a small spray bottle and fill it with undiluted white vinegar—you can easily spray surfaces for cleaning. Vinegar is also handy for disinfecting laundry, such as placing a cup of it in with your underwear which you should wash separately or by hand. Finally, allow your clothes to air dry, there's generally no need for a dryer— you'll save money and spend less time going back and forth to the clothes dryer. Both good habits I've learned from the Chinese.

61. Each of us has a spirit within us, which Marcus called a 'daemon'. Let yourself remain in contact with this spirit, this god, this drive you have as a human being. It is the part of you that is wounded and impatient when you act poorly or hurt others. Do not neglect it as it will always lead you in the right direction. Have you lost the ability to find it? Do you feel disconnected from it? Very well, I will remind you where it may be found. At all times, when you are at your most quiet and have shut off your minds jabbering, there you will find it. It will not be the part of you that is afraid or lonely or hungry or having any other appetites. Rather, it is the part of you which looks around yourself wanting nothing—content as you are in this moment and contemplating the good life. Do not confuse it with other states which will drag you through tunnels of mistakes and regrets. And if you do, climb up and right yourself and carry on.

62. Rise early that you may see the burning red sun. See how different it is in the early morning than the middle of the day? You know that it is in fact the same object and that the only reason it appears different is because of that which lies between you and it. You know that what you see is bent and changed by what lies between you. Do you know how much this same situation resembles many things in your life? Your wife, your lover, your friends, how much of them do you really see and what is influenced by what lies between? Contemplate this and hold the thought with you when you are with them—keep these thoughts close before you put them on too high a pedestal or condemn them for their errors. We are all

beacons of light. We let only part of that light show, more or less, and even less is often seen by others.

63. Men make themselves overly concerned with women and what opinions women may have of them. They dance around, trying to impress, while making themselves loathsome. Why do this? Stand at ease. Feel the nervous tension you have because you find her attractive, but do not let it rule you. When you have nothing to lose from her lack of interest you will have no nervousness.

64. Make time for yourself, your goals, and your projects. Even an hour a day is useful and if you can manage more all the better. If you do not lay aside this time, it will escape you slowly like a dripping faucet—barely perceptible, yet over time it fills an ocean. Let this ocean of time be put to your best use. Morning is an excellent time because you are fresh and because it is quiet, or at least quieter. See to it that your family respects this time and allows for it as well. They should understand that you need it for contemplation, rejuvenation and growth.

65. Do what you must do and follow your own path. You may find that you feel compelled to follow the footsteps of others, perhaps those you admire. Yet, over time those steps feel burdensome, or awkward, and perhaps they cause you injury for you have fallen. Internally you have a guide which knows what you need from moment to moment. Will you hear it? Always ask yourself: Is this what I want or what I need? Can I have both? Do I need both?

66. Consider that you are but an animal, a creature, an organism on this earth. Consider how much you have in common with the monkey, the dog, even the amoeba. How can we consider ourselves special and worthy of any favors from life? That we have managed to live this long, in one piece, is a miracle. When our day comes to resign from life we should be content knowing how far we have come. We should appreciate fully our consciousness, our ability to think and to reason. As we fully appreciate these faculties we can no longer destroy them as we had done before. Likewise, we cannot act as children and expect something different for ourselves than have come from others before use. Neither should we seek out fame or

some appreciation from others. Take stock of yourself—your strengths and weaknesses—be honest in this and move forward a little each day. Do not expect to conquer your dreams on the first shot or on the first day. Let every day be a test that you may pass by setting goals and achieving them one by one. In this way you will feel yourself progress. Is there an endpoint at which you would stop that process? If so you will have stamped out all that made you grow and become the man you are. Stick to this and do not allow yourself to waiver, no matter what happens.

67. Every moment holds the key to your salvation and equal opportunity to obtain it. It is a slippery thing which you see one moment and lose the next. This is because you have thought of it as a thing. Yet, now you have learned that it is but a way of being and that each day you must renew your oath and vow to better living. When you wake you see a million things which you could do. How often have you stood at their feet unable to decide where you will go? What will you pay attention to today? Firstly you must recognize what is your priority and that which is most important to you and your salvation. When you realize this the rest will fall into place. Remove your judgments which have colored all that you have done and all you see. They are like a chain around your neck, which is tied to horses, leading you astray. Put the chain down and walk free. Put your energy into that thing which saves you and build a strong base. Notice that when you try to juggle too many things you inevitably lose your concentration and drop something. Is it a great calamity? Perhaps not, yet you would prefer to not waste your efforts. Therefore, do not juggle. Be like the master craftsman who uses one tool at a time and plods on at his own pace—there is no rush and no reason to rush. Recognize how often you have cut yourself and done a disservice to your aims by rushing.

68. Notice how the plant grows towards light, how it maneuvers itself around obstacles to obtain light, how it sacrifices parts of itself so that the whole may live. Learn the lesson in that, and live by it.

69. When the race is finished, stop running. When a new race begins, run. Put down your tools when your work is done and do not labor further.

70. Make your bed each morning. Read some guiding stoic words each day, preferably in the morning, to set your mind straight to your tasks. Often you may find yourself with many options for which to choose. You may spend much time considering which one to endeavor upon, and after a long period of debate realize that time has escaped you while you went back and forth in your mind. That time is gone forever. Therefore, sharpen your mind to a point as early in the morning as you can, and focus on what it is you want to do. Before you sleep, think on the next day. Make lists if this will help guide you and keep you on track. Overall, remember that it is better to focus on and do one thing well with all of your concentration than to juggle many things in your mind and do none of them, or to do a few of them poorly.

71. Men are deceived by their misguided beliefs. Beliefs in longevity and permanence, in comfort and prestige. What matters most in a man's life is what he does after he realizes the futility and pointlessness of existence. Nothing you do will last, as nothing that others do will last. All things fade in time. Yet, it is this moment which matters and each of us has the opportunity to spread light and knowledge in order to limit the suffering of ourselves and our fellow humans. In this respect a man may live well and make an impact, if only for the moment. Whatever good he may do may not last very long. Therefore, he must do his best to increase the good for the moment, with an eye to the future, yet with the understanding of his impermanence.

72. Teach men how to think, not what to think, though they may despise you for it.

73. Let your face reflect the soul that resides within you. If your spirit is contemplative, let your whole being embody that feeling of inquiry and do not labor on another face. If your spirit is light and cheerful, let your whole being embody that feeling of levity and do not labor on another face. If your spirit is mournful, let your whole being embody that feeling of pain and do not labor on another face. Whatever state you find yourself in, embody and accept it with a curious and welcoming spirit. No matter what may trouble you, it will

pass in time. Do not struggle against things you may not change, but accept them. Weave them into your core and learn from them until they are a part of you. Let your psyche grow in this way, let your spirit thrive in your own existence, whatever befalls you. In this way you may overcome anything.

There is nothing greater a man can do than face his life with honest inquiry from moment to moment; than allowing himself to feel fully all that happens to him; than allowing himself to rise up to his challenges and better himself; than allowing himself to disconnect from what isn't useful and that which doesn't work; than allowing himself to be happy or to be sad; than allowing himself to rest when he needs rest and to be active the rest of the time, if only with his mind; than allowing himself to help others, once he has helped himself; than allowing himself to fail and learn from the failure; than allowing himself to break from traditions which hold no meaning and to seek out ones which do, perhaps ones long abandoned with good intentions but without good reason; than allowing himself to work hard and to understand that this is what he was put on earth for; than allowing himself to be cheerful in the face of calamities which once would have tortured him, for now he sees their inevitability; than allowing himself to break free from the bonds which once chained him to his old self, those bonds being mental and physical, and his own to keep or set aside; than allowing himself to stop when stopping is the right thing to do; than allowing himself to be confused and lost if only he is honest with himself about these things, and only if he seeks to remedy his situation; than allowing himself to be a good and honest steward of his mind, body, and spirit, even if others deride his efforts; than allowing himself to start from nothing and build gradually, without concerns for keeping up with others; than allowing himself to see straight, hear straight, and think straight, though the crowd may urge him to be crooked; than allowing himself to be his own master, for remember that Seneca counsels us thus, "We Stoics are not subjects of a despot; each of us lays claim to his own freedom". Therefore, lay claim to your freedom and live as a new man: begin today.

CPSIA information can be obtained at www.ICGtesting.com
Printed in the USA
LVOW12s2154110714

394044LV00004B/110/P